RACIAL JUSTICE IN AMERICA

HISTORIES

DESEGREGATION
and
INTEGRATION

KEVIN P. WINN WITH KELISA WING

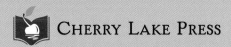
Cherry Lake Press

Published in the United States of America by Cherry Lake Publishing Group
Ann Arbor, Michigan
www.cherrylakepublishing.com

Reading Adviser: Beth Walker Gambro, MS, Ed., Reading Consultant, Yorkville, IL
Content Adviser: Kelisa Wing
Book Design and Cover Art: Felicia Macheske

Photo Credits: Library of Congress/Photo by Jack Delano, LOC Control No.; 2017796679, 7; Library of Congress/Photo by John T. Bledsoe, LOC Control No.: 2003654358, 11; © fizkes/Shutterstock.com, 13; Library of Congress/Photo by Thomas J. O'Halloran, LOC Control No.: 2003654389, 15; © Monkey Business Images/Shutterstock, 17, 24, 30; Library of Congress/Photo by Arthur S. Siegel, LOC Control No.: 2017844754, 19; Library of Congress/Photo by John T. Bledsoe, LOC Control No.: 2009632339, 20: Library of Congress/Photo by Carol M. Highsmith, LOC Control No.: 2020722855, 23; © LightField Studios/Shutterstock, 27; © iofoto/Shutterstock, 28;

Graphics Throughout: © debra hughes/Shutterstock.com; © Natewimon Nantiwat/Shutterstock.com

Library of Congress Cataloging-in-Publication Data

Names: Winn, Kevin P., author. | Wing, Kelisa, author.
Title: Desegregation and integration / Kevin P. Winn, Kelisa Wing.
Description: Ann Arbor, Michigan : Cherry Lake Publishing, [2022] | Series: Racial justice in America: Histories | Includes index. | Audience: Grades: 4-6 | Summary: "The Racial Justice in America: Histories series explores moments and eras in America's history that have been ignored or misrepresented in education due to racial bias. Desegregation and Integration explores the intents and effects of both concepts—especially as it relates to schools and education--in a comprehensive, honest, and age-appropriate way. Developed in conjunction with educator, advocate, and author Kelisa Wing to reach children of all races and encourage them to approach our history with open eyes and minds. Books include 21st Century Skills and content, as well as activities created by Wing. Also includes a table of contents, glossary, index, author biography, sidebars, educational matter, and activities"— Provided by publisher.
Identifiers: LCCN 2021010763 (print) | LCCN 2021010764 (ebook) | ISBN 9781534187450 (hardcover) | ISBN 9781534188853 (paperback) | ISBN 9781534190252 (pdf) | ISBN 9781534191655 (ebook)
Subjects: LCSH: Segregation—United States—Juvenile literature. | School integration—United States—Juvenile literature. | United States—Race relations—Juvenile literature.
Classification: LCC E184.A1 W525 2022 (print) | LCC E184.A1 (ebook) | DDC 305.800973—dc23
LC record available at https://lccn.loc.gov/2021010763
LC ebook record available at https://lccn.loc.gov/2021010764

Cherry Lake Publishing Group would like to acknowledge the work of the Partnership for 21st Century Learning, a Network of Battelle for Kids. Please visit *http://www.battelleforkids.org/networks/p21* for more information.

Printed in the United States of America

Kevin P. Winn is a children's book writer and researcher. He focuses on issues of racial justice and educational equity in his work. In 2020, Kevin earned his doctorate in Educational Policy and Evaluation from Arizona State University.

Kelisa Wing honorably served in the U.S. Army and has been an educator for 14 years. She is the author of *Promises and Possibilities: Dismantling the School to Prison Pipeline*, *If I Could: Lessons for Navigating an Unjust World*, and *Weeds & Seeds: How to Stay Positive in the Midst of Life's Storms*. She speaks both nationally and internationally about discipline reform, equity, and student engagement. Kelisa lives in Northern Virginia with her husband and two children.

CHAPTER 1

Desegregation and Integration: What's the Difference?

Sometimes, when we talk about desegregation and integration, we think they mean the same thing. They don't. The two terms are quite different.

Desegregation is the process of making sure different racial groups can share the same space. For example, in school desegregation during the 1950s and 1960s, people worked hard to eliminate single-race schools. Activists didn't think it was fair that kids couldn't meet and interact with students of different races. They also didn't think it was fair that White kids received more resources than non-White students.

Integration is different from desegregation. It refers to the relationships people form with each other after they are desegregated. Even when a school, a store, or a neighborhood is desegregated, it might not mean it is integrated. Sometimes, when people of different races share the same space, they don't always become friends or interact with each other. This means we are desegregated, but we aren't integrated.

Desegregation without integration hurts everyone. When we avoid people of other races, we are missing out. We learn from each other. We become better people when we form strong relationships with one another. Unfortunately, much of the United States doesn't have true integration, and we are becoming more segregated in many ways.

CHAPTER 2

Segregation's History

In 1863, Abraham Lincoln signed the Emancipation Proclamation. It said that slavery was illegal, but some White people in the South didn't want slavery to end. They found ways to fight against the proclamation. They made life difficult for BIPOC—Black, Indigenous, and other people of color. These actions included passing laws that made it illegal for Black people to share the same spaces as White people. This group of laws became known as Jim Crow segregation.

Under Jim Crow segregation, White people said that Black people couldn't shop in the same stores or sit in the front of buses. Different races couldn't share water fountains or swimming pools. Most importantly, they couldn't go to the same schools.

The United States Supreme Court supported Jim Crow segregation. In 1896, the Court decided that legal segregation was acceptable. The case was called *Plessy v. Ferguson*. The Supreme Court justices stated that "separate but equal" was okay. This meant that as long as different racial groups had the same resources, it was legal to keep them away from each other.

What are some reasons "separate but equal" is unjust?

White people throughout the United States created their own meaning of "separate but equal." It was obvious that their separation from Black people and other racial groups wasn't equal. This was clear in public schools. White schools received more money from the government. They had more educational resources.

As this system continued, Black people and some White people saw segregation as unfair. They didn't believe it was okay for Black schools to receive fewer resources. They fought to overturn the idea that "separate but equal" was acceptable. So, in 1954, the Supreme Court heard another case, *Brown v. Board of Education of Topeka*.

Other racial groups couldn't attend schools with White people, including Native Americans, Asians, and Mexican Americans. In 1947, Mexican Americans challenged school segregation in a legal case called *Mendez v. Westminster*. They won the case. The ruling led to statewide desegregation in California.

This time, the Supreme Court ruled that "separate educational facilities are inherently unequal." In other words, separate could never be equal.

The Supreme Court ordered schools to desegregate with the *Brown v. Board of Education* decision. Schools could no longer only serve students of only one race. At the time, this decision was a huge win for equality. It showed that the United States might begin to equalize.

However, the words the Supreme Court used in its ruling made it easy for White people to resist desegregation. The court ruled that schools should desegregate "at all deliberate speed." What did this mean? Well, no one really knew. The decision didn't say that schools should desegregate by a specific date. There were no real consequences if schools didn't desegregate. White people used the unclear language to their advantage.

Throughout the United States, White people fought against desegregation. They were especially loud about it in the South. White people protested. They were violent.

In 1960, 6-year-old Ruby Bridges became the first Black child to attend a previously all-White school in Louisiana. In fact, she was the first child to integrate schools in the entire South. White adults protested in front of the school and screamed at the first grader. The U.S. government had to step in. Federal marshals escorted Ruby into school in front of hundreds of angry White onlookers. The news captured this hatred on TV. It was broadcast around the world. For the first time ever, people in other countries saw the racist hatred that existed in the United States—the supposed land of the free.

Linda Carol Brown was a third grader. The closest school to her was a White school. The Topeka, Kansas, school district wouldn't allow her to attend this school because she was Black. Her dad, along with 12 other parents, fought against this rule. The Supreme Court agreed with Linda's dad. In 1954, it ruled that separate was unequal.

In 1959, people in Little Rock, Arkansas, protested the "Little Rock Nine," a group of nine Black students admitted to the White high school.

The World Is Watching

After World War II, the United States was in the Cold War against the Soviet Union. It was not like other wars. The United States and the Soviet Union competed in everything—for control in other countries, in sports, in science, and in military strength. The United States supported democracy—the idea that all citizens have a say in their government. Meanwhile, Russia supported communism, which wanted everyone to be economically equal but gave the government control over all property and businesses.

In the 1950s, television became more popular. For the first time, people throughout the world saw White people treating Black people like second-class citizens on the news. They started to think that the United States didn't practice what it preached.

Many experts believe that if the rest of the world hadn't been watching the United States, *Brown v. Board of Education* may not have happened. By ruling that segregation is never equal, the United States looked good in front of the world.

In May 2020, the killing of George Floyd was communicated quickly via cell phones and social media. This allowed people to respond and protest immediately.

CHAPTER 3

What Did School Desegregation Look Like?

School desegregation was an uphill battle. Many White people fought it at every chance they could. There were times when protests against desegregation were obvious. But White people were also sneaky in avoiding desegregating their schools. For example, schools used upper-level classes, like honors and advanced placement, to keep out Black students. All students would take placement tests. Even when Black students performed better than White students, they wouldn't be allowed into these classes.

Desegregation had many negative effects on Black people. Black students were forced to switch schools, but White children were not. Black students had to travel by bus for long periods of time each day to attend the desegregated schools. White students were rarely bused without a choice.

In 1959, Prince Edward County in Virginia closed all public schools to keep Black students out. White parents formed their own private schools. For 5 years, some Black students didn't have the opportunity to receive an education. Schools remained closed until 1964 when the Supreme Court said the closure was against the law.

While public schools were closed to avoid integration, Black students had to find ways to learn on their own.

Although Black schools provided an excellent education for their students, their resources were limited. The reason why Black parents and teachers wanted desegregated schools was so that they could receive equitable resources. It wasn't because they needed their children to sit next to White students in class. Black people knew they would never receive the resources they deserved without desegregation.

Somewhere between 30 and 90 percent of all Black teachers in the United States lost their jobs during desegregation. This was because White parents didn't want their children to be taught by Black teachers. School district leaders didn't think Black people were as qualified to be teachers as White people. They replaced Black teachers with White teachers.

What's the difference between equitable and equal? *Equitable* means that everyone gets what they need, while *equal* means everyone receives the same amount.

Black Teachers Matter

All students benefit from having diverse teachers. Black boys who come from families with low incomes are 39 percent less likely to drop out of high school when they have at least one Black teacher between third and fifth grade.

What are some reasons a diverse teaching staff is beneficial for all students?

CHAPTER 4

Why Are We Still Segregated Today?

Many parts of U.S. society remain segregated. People of different races often stay separated from one another. This can be seen in places like neighborhoods, churches, and schools. Just as *Brown v. Board of Education* ruled, separate is unequal.

Activists fought for desegregation and integration, but many White leaders made laws to prevent these things from happening. One way was through housing. After WWII, the government encouraged building Whites-only communities. They prevented Black people from living in White neighborhoods by not letting Black people receive loans to buy homes.

The United States has a long history of White people barring Black people from living in the same neighborhoods.

White people in business and government use falsehoods to slow integration.

Other laws and practices gave White people advantages. This includes what is called redlining. Redlining is when governments and businesses only help certain groups of people—usually White—based on incorrect assumptions about Black people. For example, many banks give loans to White people, but they refuse to give Black people those same loans. Although redlining was outlawed, it continues to negatively affect communities of color. Access to goods and services like health care and grocery stores continues to be limited in urban areas with large BIPOC populations. And communities that were redlined in the 1930s were some of the hardest hit by COVID-19 in 2020.

In 1935, the government tore down an integrated neighborhood in Cambridge, Massachusetts. It replaced the integrated housing with new buildings called housing projects. The government let only White people live in the Newtowne Court project. Only Black people could live in the Washington Elms project. This undid desegregation and integration efforts in Cambridge.

CHAPTER 5

What Does Segregation and Integration Look Like Today?

Unfortunately, many White families wish to remain segregated. They don't want their children to attend school with BIPOC students. Some White families move to other cities or suburbs with large White populations. This is called White flight. White families leave racially and economically diverse areas in search of Whiter and wealthier areas. School districts around the country have split. Often, White families try to secede from the district and form their own district. By doing this, they work to make sure their children get more money and resources in the schools. This leaves the district they left with less money.

White flight from Detroit in the 1960s left the city with decades
of financial, governmental, and educational damage to repair.

Money follows students into their schools. When families remove kids from schools, the original school loses that money. Look at your own district. How much money does each student receive? How much money would your school lose if one student left? What about 10 students?

When students flock to one school over another, the funding gap between the two schools grows and grows.

Even after *Brown v. Board of Education*, schools have segregated again. This time, schools are segregated both by race and class—meaning that kids from wealthier families usually are concentrated in schools. Sadly, this often occurs along racial lines as well.

Activists fought for more resources during *Brown v. Board of Education*. They knew that schools receive unfair differences in funding. That was a problem in the 1960s and is still a problem today. As of 2019, school districts with 75 percent or more White students receive $23 billion more than districts with 75 percent or more BIPOC students, even though they serve the same number of students.

The civil rights movement took place in the 1960s. Those efforts helped desegregate schools. That work is being undone right now. Historians believe that schools are now more racially and economically segregated than they were during official segregation.

CHAPTER 6

Desegregation Does Not Mean Integration

Even when we are desegregated—or share the same spaces with other races—it doesn't mean we are integrated. Martin Luther King Jr. once said that desegregation without integration "gives us a society where men are physically desegregated and spiritually segregated, where elbows are together and hearts are apart. It gives us special togetherness and spiritual apartness." This means that even when we may be in the same place, we may not be integrated. We need to form relationships with each other to be integrated.

People say that U.S. society won't be integrated until our kitchen tables are integrated. Building meaningful relationships with people of races other than our own helps everyone. Examples include sharing a meal together and talking with each other.

Communication is a good way to encourage integration.

Your own neighborhood may feel comfortable, but experiencing new places and making friends outside your community is an important part of life!

Why do these things matter today? Why should we be concerned that we are segregated and not integrated? There are many reasons. In schools, both Black and White students have more success when integration happens. Black students perform better on tests and make more money throughout their lives. This isn't necessarily because they are sitting next to White students. It is because schools with more White students usually receive more resources and money. White students do better too. They learn more about race and racism. They develop better relationships with people throughout their lives and are more empathetic.

What does your school look like? What does your classroom look like? What about your neighborhood? Why do you think it looks this way? What can you do to encourage integration?

There are advantages for every race when we are integrated. We learn from each other. We value one another's backgrounds rather than fear them. Even though where we came from might be different, and these differences should be valued and celebrated, we also can appreciate the humanness of one another.

Using what you learned in this book, can you explain the difference between desegregation and integration to a family member?

SHOW WHAT YOU KNOW

Does your school have a multiracial club? Multiracial clubs are a great way to truly get to know the backgrounds of others and integrate. For this show what you know assignment, research whether or not your school has a multiracial club where students of different backgrounds can get together, learn from one another, and create meaningful friendships. Even if your school's student body is primarily one race, share how multicultural clubs can help with integration. If your school does have one, how can you and others get more involved? What can you do to help create such a club if it doesn't exist?

Do you know there are so many different ways to show what you know? Rather than using traditional ways to display knowledge, try something new to complete this assignment. Here are some ideas:

1. Rap
2. Mural
3. Musical
4. Debate
5. Web page
6. Speech
7. Bulletin board
8. Jigsaw puzzle
9. Show and tell
10. Essay
11. Diorama
12. Performance
13. Podcast
14. Journal
15. OR add your own...

EXTEND YOUR LEARNING

Learning for Justice
learningforjustice.org

GLOSSARY

activists (AK-tih-vists) people who work for a cause

communism (KAHM-yuh-nih-zuhm) a system of government where the government owns all businesses and property and resources are meant to be divided equally

concentrated (KON-suhn-tray-tuhd) grouped into one place

democracy (dih-MOK-ruh-see) a form of government where citizens elect people to represent them to make laws

desegregation (dee-seg-ruh-GAY-shuhn) the process of trying to make sure different racial groups can share the same space

empathetic (em-puh-THEH-tik) compassionate toward others

equitable (eh-kwuh-tuh-buhl) when everyone receives what they need

federal marshals (FED-ur-uhl MAHR-shuhls) people who work in U.S. law enforcement within the Department of Justice

integration (in-tuh-GRAY-shuhn) the relationships people form with each other after desegregation

Jim Crow segregation (JIHM CROH seg-ruh-GAY-shuhn) a system of laws that separated White people from other races, especially Black people

racial groups (RAY-shuhl GROOPS) people who share similar traits based on physical and social similarities

redlining (RED-lyne-ing) not providing a person a home loan or other service based on race or other types of discrimination

resist (rih-ZIST) to withstand or go against

secede (sih-SEED) to formally leave a group

INDEX